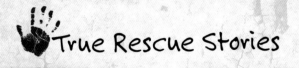
True Rescue Stories

True Ocean Rescue Stories

Susan Jankowski

Enslow Publishers, Inc.
40 Industrial Road
Box 398
Berkeley Heights, NJ 07922
USA

http://www.enslow.com

Library of Congress Cataloging-in-Publication Data

Jankowski, Susan.

True ocean rescue stories / Susan Jankowski.

p. cm. —(True rescue stories)

Includes index.

Summary: "Readers will learn about some of greatest sea rescues including the Mary Rose, the Peter Iredale, the Britannic, the Squalus, and the U.S. Coast Guard"—Provided by publisher.

ISBN 978-0-7660-3665-9

1. Shipwrecks—Juvenile literature. 2. Boating accidents—Juvenile literature. 3. Search and rescue operations—Juvenile literature. I. Title.

GR525.J36 2010

910.4'52—dc22   2010003846

Printed in the United States of America

082010 Lake Book Manufacturing, Inc., Melrose Park, IL

10 9 8 7 6 5 4 3 2 1

To Our Readers: We have done our best to make sure all Internet addresses in this book were active and appropriate when we went to press. However, the author and the Publisher have no control over, and assume no liability for, the material available on those Internet sites or on other Web sites they may link to. Any comments or suggestions can be sent by e-mail to comments@enslow.com or to the address on the back cover.

Enslow Publishers, Inc., is committed to printing our books on recycled paper. The paper in every book contains 10% to 30% post-consumer waste (PCW). The cover board on the outside of each book contains 100% PCW. Our goal is to do our part to help young people and the environment too!

Photo Credits: Shutterstock.com

Cover Illustration: Shutterstock.com

Contents

Ocean Rescue Facts

French underwater explorer Jacques Yves Cousteau and engineer Emile Gagnan invented the Aqua-Lung, a compressed-air device for breathing underwater, in 1943. Today it is known as SCUBA gear; these letters stand for "self-contained underwater breathing apparatus."

Cape Disappointment is at the southwest corner of Washington State. The U.S. Coast Guard responds to 400 distress calls per year here. Coast Guard rescue teams have nicknamed the spot "Cape D."

To make a waterway safer for ships to pass through, engineers use special equipment to scoop up mud, rocks, or sand from its bottom. This is called "dredging."

The U.S. Department of Defense created the Global Navigation Satellite System (GNSS). It became available for use by citizens in the early 1980s. Since then sailors and pilots have been able to use Global Positioning Systems (GPS) for navigation. The U.S. Air Force now controls this satellite.

During the past five years, African pirates have taken ship captains hostage off the coast of Somalia, in the Gulf of Aden, and also in the Indian Ocean. They hold the hostages for ransom money. Naval ships from the United States, Canada, France, and other countries are patrolling the area to try to protect the ships from pirates.

A jetty is a wall built out into the water to slow the current to help ships pass through an area.

A sailor, or seaman, is also called a mariner. "Maritime" means having to do with the sea.

For a half-century, specially trained Navy Seals have risked their lives to destroy underwater mines, prepare areas for an attack, or spy to gather information on the enemy. They are some of the most skilled divers in the world.

Ships in the air and at sea can send out radio waves to find the location and distance of other ships and objects using radar systems. The term "radar" comes from the words, "Radio Direction and Ranging."

Sharks can mistake a person on a surfboard for a sea lion, which is one of the animals they hunt. There are about five great white shark attacks each year across the globe.

A sonar device locates other ships or objects by sending out sound waves that bounce back to it. It is especially useful in locating submarines.

Mariners learned from the mistakes made by the builders and crew of the *Titanic*, which sunk in the Atlantic Ocean. Among the most important lessons is that a ship must have enough lifeboat seats for every passenger on board.

Chapter 1

The King's Favorite: The *Mary Rose*

On a clear, summer day in 1545, French raiders approached the English Isle of Wight. King Henry Tudor VIII expected the crew of the *Mary Rose* to use its ship's awesome firepower to stop the French attack. With fanfare, the king arrived at his Southsea Castle in Portsmouth to watch his favorite ship set sail for another battle with the French. The water was calm because there was no wind. But this causes problems for sailing vessels, which need moving air to push them forward.

What the Sea Wants, the Sea Will Have

About one mile out to sea, the *Mary Rose* faced enemy fire. Upon her firing at the French, water flooded into the *Mary Rose's* open gun ports. Her lower deck quickly took on water. From atop his castle one mile away, King Henry watched in horror as his prized ship began to sink!

On board, the ship was mayhem. The *Mary Rose* had been overloaded with supplies, extra sailors, and large guns called "cannon." This made it hard for sailors to move around as the ship took on water. It also made the ship heavier and less likely to stay afloat.

Some of the sailors were from other countries like Spain and did not speak English. This meant the crew could not talk—or shout—information to each other to try to stop the ship from sinking. They were likely yelling things such as, "Close the ports! Stop the water!" but in different languages. Crew members couldn't understand what their shipmates were saying.

Sailors were trapped beneath nets that had been stretched out on the lower decks to keep enemies from sneaking on board. As the water poured in, frantic sailors clawed at these nets to try to escape. Only this caused them to become more tangled in the nets.

Worst of all, most of the sailors did not know how to swim. Four centuries ago, people did not always make it a point to learn. In fact, many sailors avoided it. "What the sea wants, the sea will have," is an old saying. Back then, people believed that there was never a good reason to go into the water; it was always best to avoid it. To jump into the water to learn how to swim would be risking your life, they felt. You would be testing your fate!

To The Towers!

A shocked King Henry watched from his castle as seven hundred people drowned in the Atlantic Ocean. Still, about thirty people survived! These lucky folks were on the upper deck when the ship began to sink. As the waves of the Atlantic swallowed the deck, they were able to climb onto the ship's towers. They hung on to the towers with all their might while listening to the screams of shipmates perishing on the decks below.

One of the highest ranking officers on the *Mary Rose* was Vice Admiral Sir George Carew. His uncle, Sir Gawain Carew, was on a nearby sister ship as the *Mary Rose* began to sink. Sir Gawain later wrote in his journal about the day the *Mary Rose* went down.

After he learned the *Mary Rose* was taking on water, Sir Gawain called out to his nephew. "George! George!" The sound of his voice mixed with men's shouts over the roar of the ocean.

Soon it became clear that things were dire. Sir Gawain asked his nephew what was happening.

"They are the sort of knaves whom I cannot rule!" George had called back to his uncle. This meant crew members didn't know what to do to save the ship—or themselves. That was the last time the two men ever spoke. That evening, Sir George was pulled underwater by the force of the mighty Atlantic.

To the people on the towers, it must have seemed like a long time until their sister ship could get close enough to the *Mary Rose* to pull them out. What a relief it was to be pulled from the waves by their mates!

From the top of his castle on shore, King Henry must have felt helpless as he watched the sea swallow up his beloved *Mary Rose*. His servants must have also had a hard time watching hundreds of people, unable to swim, vanish beneath the waves.

A Proud King's Prized Ship

Henry Tudor was only eighteen when he was crowned King Henry VIII. This meant he became head of England's army and navy and its fleet of ships. Since England was at war with France, he felt it was best to build up the country's military. This meant building new ships for battles at sea. The king had paid special attention to the *Mary Rose*.

As a young man, King Henry was handsome, charming, and strong. He threw grand parties. He danced with ladies of high society to songs he wrote himself. He was a good athlete and liked to play sports. He held many tennis, hunting, archery, and jousting contests. In the early years of his reign, the young king seemed to enjoy his rule.

By the time he was in his fifties, King Henry's life was not so carefree. Years of eating too much had made him overweight. At the time of the *Mary Rose* sinking, Henry's son and heir, Edward VI, had been born in 1537. His demand for that male heir led him to marry six different women. The king became infamous for having two of them beheaded.

One of the few things the aging king could still be proud of was his naval fleet. Of these, the *Mary Rose* was his favorite. He had named it after his younger sister as well as the Tudor family emblem, the rose. Like many sixteenth-century vessels, the *Mary Rose* had high towers at the bow and stern, so it looked like a floating castle.

Yet the *Mary Rose* was a warship. It was one of the first ships with gun ports cut out along the sides of the hull. It was one of the first ships to be able to fire a full broadside of cannons. English sailors could fire sixty light guns and twenty heavy guns through these ports, which were small, window-like openings. ("Guns" was the word sailors used for what people today call "cannon.")

The king enjoyed showing off the *Mary Rose* to his people and visitors. He especially liked its show of strength as a warship when fighting enemies from Scotland and France. The Atlantic Ocean and nearby seas were dangerous waters during this time. Crews were always watching for ships. In one of her early battles, the crew of the *Mary Rose* blasted a French flagship and destroyed its mast. This was a sign of defeat for the French fleet. It was a victory for England.

"The Fairest Flower That Ever Sailed"

Even though it was made for battle, the *Mary Rose* was also a luxury vessel. The king wanted the *Mary Rose* to have the best of everything. Her kitchen was well-stocked with beef, lamb, venison (deer meat), cod fish, and barrels of fruit and other supplies. Nobles on the ship used the best silver when dining. The cabins of the *Mary Rose* were filled with games and

Swimming For Their Lives

Sailors of old saw no reason to go into the water. They believed the saying, "What the sea wants, the sea will have." This meant many people did not learn how to swim. Today most people know that swimming is an important skill that can help a person survive.

There are many ways people in the United States learn to swim. Some schools include swimming classes as part of their physical education programs. This means students receive a grade from their gym teacher for their mastery of swimming skills. Other people learn to swim at community centers and pools in public parks. There are also swim coaches and classes at private health clubs.

There are different strokes to learn. "Treading water" is one the first things beginners learn, because it helps a person stay afloat. But in cold water, rescue experts say it's best to try to float with legs together and arms folded at the chest to keep in body heat.

Whether a person is an expert or novice, it is never safe to swim alone. Always bring a friend. Or swim where there is a lifeguard on duty in case something goes wrong in the water. Even good swimmers should wear life jackets whenever they are on a boat. This helps keep the person afloat when in the water for long periods. It can also prevent an injured or tired person from being pulled under by strong currents. Finally, it is important to obey "No Swimming or Diving" signs wherever they are posted. This means the waters are too dangerous for swimmers or too shallow for divers.

musical instruments. The king fondly called the *Mary Rose*, "The fairest flower of all ships that ever sailed." It was as though the *Mary Rose* had become a symbol of King Henry VIII's reign!

Maritime Mystery

To this day, people are not sure what caused the *Mary Rose* to sink. The ship has since been salvaged. Experts are studying its remains. Many believe a squall came up, which is a sudden gust of wind that makes big waves. Perhaps the surprise storm made a wave large enough to cause the ship, overloaded with sailors and supplies, to capsize.

Some believe the ship took too sharp of a turn with her gun ports open. The open ports may have been too close to the surface of the water. When this happened, sailors may not have been able to understand each other as they tried to solve the problem. The French Navy also claimed to have sunk it.

Because the *Mary Rose* sank in a place where the bottom is made of silt, she is well-preserved. Millions watched her salvage operation on TV. Today, the *Mary Rose* is docked at Portsmouth Historic Dockyard in the United Kingdom. A museum displaying items found on the ship is open to visitors.

Chapter 2

The Wreck and Rescue of the *Peter Iredale*

Great Britain was one of the nations doing business with America by sea trade in the early 1900s. Many companies paid for big ships to transport their goods across the globe. The *Peter Iredale*, which was a small sailing vessel called a "bark," was among these.

Ports in America's Pacific Northwest were crowded with ships carrying fish, timber, and farm crops. Ships hauled cargo down the Columbia River to its mouth at the Pacific Ocean. From here, ocean vessels could carry the cargo to other countries. The *Peter Iredale* traveled from Britain to the shores of Mexico during the summer of 1906. It continued on to California and finally, north to Oregon that fall. Its mission was to pick up a shipment of wheat and carry it back to Great Britain.

Saved By A Captain's Quick Thinking

The *Peter Iredale* was built in England in 1890. It was made of steel. Like other barks of its time, it had been built with four tall masts. The British shipping company of Iredale & Porter owned the ship. This company was well-known in the city of Liverpool. Captain H. Lawrence was one of the owners of the business and the ship. He was known around town for his red beard and clever sense of humor.

On the voyage, the captain and crew may have spotted whales heading south for the winter. They surely heard the dog-like cries of seals along the Pacific Coast. A pod of dolphins could have breached from the water alongside the ship anywhere and at any time. Throughout their voyage, sea gulls circled behind the ship and begged for scraps of food.

One month later, in the dark hours of early morning, the *Peter Iredale* sailed into a heavy fog. This made navigation much harder for Captain Lawrence. He finally spotted the beam from the Tillamook Lighthouse through the low lying clouds. Because he was a skilled sailor, Captain Lawrence was able to steer the ship even in dense fog.

Then a heavy wind came up from the southeast; it

blew with great force against the ship. At the same time, the water's current picked up strength. This meant the captain had to work hard to steer and stay on course. But there was little time to turn the ship to change direction. Suddenly, the *Peter Iredale* was in the breakers! Sailors braced themselves as the ship ran aground at Clatsop Beach on the Oregon shore. The ship smashed into the sandbar so hard three of her four masts snapped in half! Yet no one on the ship was injured.

In the end, the quick thinking of Captain Lawrence saved everyone on board. Captain Lawrence ordered his crew to abandon the *Peter Iredale* right away. He also ordered his men to launch rockets to signal for help. He focused on saving his men and himself. Crew members knew how to quickly carry out the captain's orders. In this way, the captain and crew of the *Peter Iredale* saved themselves!

Rocket-Fire Rescue

Men at a lifesaving station on the shore saw the rockets shooting up into the sky. A rescue team boarded lifeboats. They set off in the direction of the rocket fire. In their small boats, the rescuers withstood the same dangerous winds, waves, and strong current as had the captain and crew of the *Peter Iredale*. Still, they managed to pick up all twenty-seven crew members and bring them to nearby Fort Stevens for care. They even saved two stowaways!

It was the rescue team's duty to save sailors in the dangerous waters of what mariners call, "The Pacific's Graveyard." Yet they had put their own lives at grave risk during the rescue. Theirs was truly a most dangerous job!

Mother Nature Takes the Blame

William K. Inman was a member of the rescue team who spoke about how Captain Lawrence acted shortly after he was rescued. Upon reaching the shore, Captain Lawrence stood stiffly at attention and saluted his ship, which was now stranded on the beach.

"May God bless you and may your bones bleach in these sands," said the captain. Then he raised the bottle of whiskey he had in his hand and said, "Boys! Have a drink."

Captain Lawrence's troubles were not yet over, however. Upon his return to England, he had to face members of the British Naval Court and answer questions about how the *Peter Iredale* became stranded. The captain was surely tired after the long, return trip back to England, which took several months. But the way he answered their questions was important. He had to remember many details. If it turned out he had made a mistake that caused the shipwreck, his career as a sea captain would be ruined. It is likely that a bad outcome would hurt his business in Liverpool, too. No one wanted to pay for a voyage that might end in lost cargo during a shipwreck caused by the captain's poor judgment.

To his relief, the court ruled the shipwreck was caused by the sudden shift in wind and strong current. It ruled Captain Lawrence was not to blame. Today, many people say it was the quick thinking of Captain Lawrence that saved the crew of the *Peter Iredale*.

A Public Attraction

Back in America, hundreds of tourists were crowding Clatsop Beach. They were there to see the remains of the *Peter Iredale*.

Just one day after the ship crashed into the sandbar, a news reporter for the *Oregon Journal* wrote, "In spite of the gale that was raging, scores flocked to the scene of the disaster." This meant people ignored stormy weather, wind, and rain. Instead, they hurried to the beach to get a look at the ship.

Graveyard of the Pacific

Thousands of ships have been pushed off course by heavy winds, high waves, and strong currents in the waters between Oregon and Washington. The place where the Pacific Ocean meets the mouth of the Columbia River is called, the "Graveyard of the Pacific", because so many shipwrecks have happened there. There have been two thousand shipwrecks in this channel since the late 1700s. This is when the U.S. government began recording wrecks at this spot. Many mariners have lost their lives in these rough waters.

Today, the beams from two lighthouses on shore help guide ship captains who travel through the channel. They are located on "Cape Disappointment," which is a peninsula (a strip of land with water on three sides) that sticks out into the channel. Its shoreline is made of jagged rocks that can slice a ship's hull upon impact.

Engineers have tried to make the waters around Cape Disappointment safer. They built a jetty, which is a wall that extends out into the water to block the force of strong currents. They have also dredged the bottom to carve out deeper spaces for ships to pass through. Still U.S. Coast Guard rescue teams remain on alert for ships in trouble.

Navigating the ocean is much safer now than it was three centuries ago. However, the basic nautical chart is still used by mariners to plot their course. Today there are more tools for this purpose. Captains use Radio Direction and Ranging (RADAR), which sends out a radio signal to find objects and other ships. A Global Positioning System (GPS) measures a ship's distance to satellites the United States has placed in orbit in outer space. If a crew needs to be rescued today, it has more than rockets to signal for help!

The journalist also reported two railroad lines, the Astoria and Columbia River railroads, planned to run trains to a station near the site. Today, tourists who visit Fort Stevens State Park in Oregon can still see the ship on the beach at its final resting place.

Chapter 3

Crew of *Titanic's* "Sister Ship" Saves Itself

Few people know that the famous *Titanic*, which struck an iceberg and sank in the Atlantic Ocean, had two sister ships in her fleet. The *Olympic* was an ocean liner that served as a passenger ship in the early 1900s. It made regular trips to and from Great Britain.

The second sister ship was the *Britannic*, built for luxury travel. But the British Royal Navy turned it into a floating hospital. Great Britain needed the *Britannic* to carry wounded soldiers and sailors in the days leading up to World War I. German U-boat submarines were prowling the deep waters of the Atlantic Ocean, as well as the Mediterranean Sea. They fired torpedoes at enemy ships and sometimes destroyed them.

Sheila MacBeth, a twenty-six-year-old Scottish nurse, boarded the *Britannic* for the sixth time on November 12, 1916. This was four years after the

Titanic sank. The ship was headed for the Mediterranean Sea, where it would pick up patients on the shores of Italy. In her diary, MacBeth wrote she was happy to be back on board the *Britannic*.

"It's such a relief to find the same cabin and room-mate…and to see how 'homely' it is now looking, with my chintz cushions and our nice jar of brown beech leaves," she had written about her cabin on the ship.

After the sinking of the *Titanic*, the British Royal Navy added safety features to the *Britannic* its famous sister ship had not had. For example, the *Britannic* had a special hull that could withstand a crash with an iceberg. Unlike the *Titanic*, there were enough lifeboat seats for every passenger on board.

Iceberg Charlie

Captain Charles Bartlett was the *Britannic's* veteran captain. He had overseen the building of the ship himself. He also had experience navigating around icebergs and avoiding torpedoes from U-boat submarines. He'd fought many battles in the North Sea for Great Britain. Some people said Bartlett's skills were so good he could "smell an iceberg." For this reason, he'd earned the nickname, "Iceberg Charlie."

The *Britannic* had three red crosses painted on its

sides and two lighted crosses atop its towers. The nations of the world had agreed not to fire upon each other's hospital ships. The *Britannic's* crosses and also her strings of lights left no doubt to anyone who saw her that she was a hospital ship. So Sheila must have felt quite safe.

To Sheila, this voyage felt a little like she was "on holiday," or on a vacation. The *Britannic* was gliding over the beautiful Aegean Sea, an arm of the Mediterranean Sea located between Greece and Turkey. When the ship stopped in Italy to load up with coal, Sheila and her friends went ashore to tour nearby villages. She wrote about their adventures. The women went Christmas shopping in Naples. They enjoyed lunches hosted by locals.

"They're 'shoveling' mounds of spaghetti!" Sheila wrote.

Finally, there were so few passengers on this voyage that Sheila and the other nurses were able to wander the ship. No "Officers Only" or "Passengers Only" signs had been posted. On most voyages, the *Britannic* was packed with doctors, nurses, and patients. It could hold over three thousand people!

Sheila wandered the *Britannic's* decks, which were lined with beds, and wondered what it would have been like if the ship not been turned into a hospital. The dining room had been turned into the intensive care unit for the most seriously wounded. The grand reception room was filled with beds for those recovering from surgery.

The day before the *Britannic* was set to pick up passengers, Sheila and others, like veteran nurse Violet Jessop, were busy preparing for patients.

"From breakfast time until our afternoon swim, we worked like factory hands, tying up all the kits for the next evening so that we might rest the day before the patients came on board," Sheila wrote.

Still the women found time for an afternoon swim and to attend a church service in the evening. Like other nurses, Sheila chose to sleep late the next morning because she knew she'd need to rest up before patients came aboard.

Women (and Children) First!

Just minutes after Sheila and the others sat down to breakfast, they heard a loud crash.

It felt like a "shiver" had passed through the ship, Sheila later wrote.

Yet Major Harold Priestly, who had taken charge of the dining room, ordered the nurses to keep eating. He did not want anyone to panic. But no one wanted to eat until everyone knew what had caused the crash. Crew members thought the *Britannic* must have hit another ship—and they felt sorry for the other ship!

Captain Bartlett thought the *Britannic* had run over an explosive mine. This is because no one had seen the trail in the water torpedoes often make. Either one could have caused the crash. The captain ordered the ship's radio operator to signal for help right away. Then he sounded the ship's sirens.

The wail of the sirens finally prompted Major Priestly to order the nurses to leave the dining room and get their things. Sheila ran back to her cabin and grabbed her coat, a pillow, and life vest. She left behind the gifts she'd bought, her purse, and all of her other belongings.

Violet Jessop had survived the sinking of the *Titanic*, as well as other shipwrecks. Although no one on the *Britannica* panicked, Violet stayed especially calm. While all of the other nurses were running back to their cabins, Violet calmly finished cooking breakfast for another nurse who was ill. She brought it to the sick nurse at her cabin and made her eat it. Then she helped her dress. Only when she was sure the sick nurse was safely ready to board a lifeboat did Violet go back to her own cabin. As a survivor, she knew the item she would want most was her toothbrush! Finally, Violet joined the others and boarded a lifeboat.

Major Priestly oversaw the evacuation of the crew and passengers to the waiting lifeboats. True to the naval custom "Women and Children First!" he ordered women on the ship to board the lifeboats before the male passengers.

Island of Safety?

Meanwhile, Captain Bartlett had spotted the Greek island of Kea. "Full speed ahead!" he had likely ordered his crew, which means turn on all engines at full force. His idea was to ground the sinking vessel in the shallow waters off the island's beach. But this caused the ship to take on more water even faster. This also made it too dangerous to lower the lifeboats full of waiting passengers! Once Captain Bartlett saw this, he gave the order to stop the engines.

But two lifeboats had already been lowered into the water without the captain's consent. Within a few seconds, they were sucked into the ship's propellers!

One of these lifeboats carried Violet Jessop. Just before her boat was sucked in, Violet leapt into the water. She began to get pulled under by the current.

Lifesaving Gear

Mariners the world-over responded to the sinking of the *Titanic* in 1912 by making a list of safety standards all ships should follow. This included a list of safety gear. They wrote the "Safety of Life At Sea" (SOLAS) treaty. They then founded the International Maritime Organization (IMO) with support from the United Nations (UN) a few decades later. Many nations signed the treaty and joined the IMO. It held its first official meeting at UN headquarters in Geneva, Switzerland in 1959.

Today, the IMO has 170 members. Its main offices are in England. About three hundred people work there to make sure mariners safely sail and tow cargo across Earth's seas.

The Australian Maritime Safety Authority (AMSA), an IMO member, has a list of safety checks captains must do before launching a vessel. Since a fire can destroy a ship, it's also up to the captain to check firefighting equipment. The captain also makes sure the all of the ship's parts, such as the electrical and communications systems, work as they should. The captain makes sure he or she can properly steer the vessel.

The AMSA has a list of lifesaving equipment that must be ready for use in an emergency. Lifeboats and rafts must be properly stowed and easily launched. Lines of rope and distress flares must be easy to reach and use. Passengers need to be trained to use life jackets and, when needed, thermal suits. Finally, every ship must have an official evacuation plan. All passengers and crew members must learn how to follow it in case the worst happens.

Things seemed bleak as Violet gasped for air and swallowed mouthfuls of seawater. She swam with all her might towards the surface. Then Violet hit her head on the keel of another lifeboat. Suddenly, a hand reached down and pulled her up to safety. Later, Violet learned she had fractured her skull when her head hit the keel of the boat. Seventy others were wounded or killed that day.

All of this happened shortly after nine o'clock in the morning. One hour later, the *Britannic* was underwater. Thirty-five lifeboats were left floating off the coast of the tiny island. Soon British warships in the area and also a Greek fishing vessel came to the rescue. By nightfall, all of the survivors were safely resting in hotels or had boarded other ships.

Over a half-century later, ocean explorer Jacques Cousteau dove off the waters of Greece to take underwater photographs of the *Britannic*. He hoped pictures might help solve the mystery of what had caused her to sink. Although the *Britannic* was still in one piece, there are holes from what looks like explosions. This leads many people to believe the *Britannic* sailed over a sea mine in the Aegean Sea.

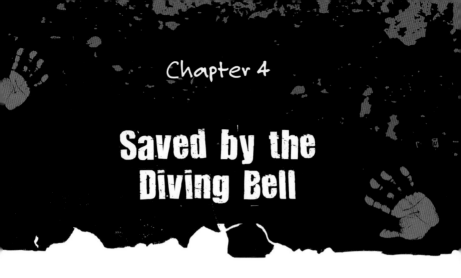

Chapter 4

Saved by the Diving Bell

Before a new submarine can become part of a naval fleet, it must pass a series of test dives. These are made in the safety of domestic waters. The tests help officers and engineers know whether equipment on the vessel is working the way it should. Then everyone can be sure the submarine is ready for long voyages or battles.

On a spring morning in May 1939, the *Squalus* began another of its many test dives off the coast of Portsmouth, New Hampshire. It looked like the sub would soon be ready to enter active duty having already passed several other tests.

Before U.S. Navy submarines ran on nuclear power, as they do today, they ran on diesel fuel and electricity. This was true of the *Squalus*. At the water's surface, its diesel engine could reach the air it needed to combust, or, "fire up." Electricity then powered the

Squalus as it cruised the oceans' depths. The sub's captain and crew relied on the electrical system when the submarine was submerged.

As the *Squalus* plunged into the depths of the Atlantic Ocean for its next test, the panel of lights sailors called, "The Christmas Tree" lit up green. This meant all air and water valves were closed. All green lights showed it was safe for the submarine to go down deep into the ocean. A red light would have meant a valve had been left open. An open valve could quickly become dangerous to a submarine, because it could let water in.

Two Heroes: Momsen and McCann

Vice Admiral Charles Bowers Momsen had been serving in the U.S. Navy since World War I. Throughout his career, Charles Momsen proved to be a hero. He was known as a man of great determination. He never gave up no matter how difficult things seemed at any given moment. He helped win sea battles for the United States Navy.

During one test, Momsen jumped into the water; swam over to a torpedo that had failed to explode; wrapped his arms around it; then hauled it back to the ship to try to find out why it had failed.

Captain Momsen was always working to protect sailors. He had the talent and skills to invent things that became useful rescue tools for the U.S. Navy. Before Jacques Cousteau invented the famous Aqua-Lung, Momsen invented the "Momsen Lung." This was a breathing device divers could use underwater for short periods. Because of this invention, sailors could abandon ship and swim to the surface.

Momsen also worked with his friend, Lieutenant Commander Allan Rockwell McCann, to invent the "diving bell." This was a pear-shaped chamber made of steel that could be raised and lowered by cables attached to a ship. About ten people could fit in the diving bell. It had a supply of air and an exhaust hose built into it so the people inside could breathe.

The two officers invented the diving bell to rescue sailors trapped in submarines. It could withstand the currents and air pressure of the deep ocean down to about eight hundred feet.

Like Momsen, McCann was very smart and good at solving problems. He had led many crews during World War I and World War II. He was known among sailors as a good leader. He had many loyal crew members; the sailors respected him. They trusted him with their lives.

The day of the *Squalus's* test dive, the two men were called by commanding officers to work together again. This time they would put their own diving bell to the test—like never before!

The Longest Hours

Within minutes after the *Squalus* submerged, there were shouts. Somehow, a valve had been left open. The engine room was flooding at a rapid speed! To save the submarine, the crew sealed off that room and the twenty-six men trapped inside all died. The surviving crew members knew they had gone down too deep in the ocean to use their Momsen Lungs to swim to the surface. They knew they had no choice but to wait to be rescued. They also knew they might run out of time before this could happen. They would soon be out of air and the temperature inside the submarine was quickly falling.

When the *Squalus* did not resurface on time, naval officers knew something was wrong. Its crew had called for help over a telephone line, which had broken. Only parts of their message could be heard. *Squalus* crew members had found a way to fire rockets. When a naval engineer above the surface saw a rocket, he sounded the alarm.

Once again, Momsen and McCann were called upon to lead the rescue. Momsen led the divers and McCann was in charge of the diving bell.

A ship carrying an untested diving bell was nearby. When the two officers heard of the submarine's plight, they ordered that nearby ship to speed to the scene.

No Air or Heat

As the submarine took on more water, chemicals mixed with other liquids. This caused the air inside the *Squalus* to become toxic. Two young sailors, Carl Bryson and Danny Perisco, were among those trying to stay alive as the *Squalus* was taking on water.

On board the sinking submarine, the men did not talk much. They needed to save air.

"One of the problems was trying to stay alive, okay? The air was bad . . . we put out all the soda lime we had to absorb the carbon dioxide . . . the main thing to do was conserve oxygen," Bryson later told a television reporter as he remembered the event.

No electricity meant there would not be any heat. The temperature inside the submarine was dropping even faster than water was coming in. Inside, the trapped sailors ate canned fruit and did what they could to keep warm.

Water Warriors

Navy divers are among the toughest, most skilled warriors in the world. They undergo intense training to prepare for special operations on the sea, in the air, or on land. This is how they got the name Navy "SEALs."

The first group of specially trained Navy SEALs was formed in 1962. Today, it is a SEAL's job to destroy underwater mines in the ocean. A SEAL may be sent into combat to spy on the enemy, rescue hostages, or quietly prepare an area for a larger attack from U.S. military forces. Some SEALs are specially trained for diving missions. Navy SEALs also salvage ships. Finally, they support military police and the U.S. Coast Guard.

When Somali pirates took over an American cargo ship in the Indian Ocean on April 7, 2009, Navy SEALs came to the rescue. The pirates took Captain Richard Phillips hostage by holding a gun to his head. The pirates' goal was to hold him for a ransom of one million dollars. After four days at sea, Captain Phillips tried to escape the pirates by jumping overboard. But the pirates recaptured him.

The next day, Navy SEAL snipers killed three of the pirates—each with a single shot fired by SEALs at the same time. This was important, because if one of the SEALs missed one of their human targets, that pirate might have enough time to grab the gun, pull the trigger, and shoot the hostage. Navy SEALs are trained to hit a target within one inch from 100 yards away within one minute. A fourth pirate the SEALs left alive surrendered. In the twenty-first century, protecting American cargo ships from pirates has become part of the Navy SEAL's mission.

The sound of the first rescue diver to reach the *Squalus* was most welcome by the men.

"I could hear the diver's feet, with his big, metal shoes. When they hit the deck, it was very clear," Persico remembered.

The diver tied a cable from the rescue chamber to the *Squalus*. Inside Persico and Bryson could hear him cursing above them; the diver was having a hard time with the cable.

Rescuers made four trips down 243 feet in the Atlantic Ocean in the diving bell. Sometimes it was slow going, because the lines to the submarine and ship often became tangled. Diver after diver went down into the dark waves to untangle the cables. Sometimes it took two or three tries before the diver had success.

Persico and Bryson were among the last of the thirty-three survivors to leave the sunken ship on the fifth and final trip of the diving bell. Divers made this last trip to check the flooded rooms for survivors. By this time, the two young sailors had been underwater for thirty-four hours.

Then their rescue in the diving bell took four more hours, because the cables kept getting tangled. Finally,

McCann gave the order to haul the diving bell up by hand.

Soon after, Momsen and McCann oversaw operations to salvage the *Squalus*. It was repaired and renamed the *Sailfish*. The vessel proved worthy of battle during World War II.

Chapter 5

By Air or By Sea: U.S. Coast Guard Saves Surfers

Die-hard surfers of the Atlantic and Pacific coasts enjoy their sport year-round. Some of America's best waves appear along parts of the Pacific Coast. Even in winter, surfers wear wet suits and brave cold waters in search of the perfect wave. Yet surfers sometimes find themselves struggling with sudden riptides and strong currents. When they are unable to swim back to shore, highly trained U.S. Coast Guard rescue teams come to their aid. Rescue teams arrive at the scene in boats and in helicopters.

When twenty-two-year-old Marciel Quiros and three friends slipped on their wet suits and paddled out into the water at Benson Beach in Washington, they saw only big waves. They looked forward to a good ride. Yet the waters off this beach are known for dangerous riptides. When a sudden strong current caught the group, they swam for shore. But Marciel was struggling. Despite his strong swimming skills, he couldn't make it to shore. His friends watched from the beach as U.S. Coast Guard rescue teams arrived in a 47-foot motorboat while a HH-60 helicopter hovered above. The motorboat reached Marciel first and pulled him from the current.

A surfer at nearby Cannon Beach in Oregon was not so lucky. In February 2009 the man paddled out to a wave but was quickly carried out far from shore. He swam with all his might and nearly made it back. But then he was pulled out to sea again. A witness on the shore saw the man and used his cell phone to call for help. Then the man vanished in the waves.

The U.S. Coast Guard crew arrived in a motorboat and spotted the man for a moment before he vanished again. Had he gone under for good? Coast Guard pilots in the helicopter above spotted the man trying to stay afloat in the rough waters. The pilot positioned the helicopter above the man. A brave rescuer attached to a cable was lowered down into the waves. The rescuer was able to grab hold of the grateful man. Crew members in the helicopter then hoisted the two men up to safety.

Dolphins Save Surfer from Great White Shark

Sometimes surfers get a little help from their animal friends. When twenty-four-year-old Todd Endris took the day off to go surfing with his friends in Monterey, California, he had no idea he was about to become part of the ocean's food chain.

One minute, he was sitting on his surfboard. In an instant, 'wham!,' a twelve-foot-long Great White shark rammed into his surfboard. Then the shark tried to get its jaws around both Todd and the board "like a sandwich," he later said. Still, Todd was able to fight off the shark by kicking it with one leg as it tried to swallow his other leg.

All of a sudden, a pod of dolphins arrived and circled the surfboard to protect Todd! By this time, everyone on the beach, including the lifeguards and Todd's friend, Brian, was worried. Some even doubted Todd would make it back alive—until the dolphins came and blocked off the shark.

Their plan worked! Although he was wounded, Todd was able to paddle his way back to shore. There a "Medivac" medical helicopter airlifted him to a hospital. Todd's back had been shredded by the shark, but because his stomach had been pressed to the surfboard when the shark tried to bite him, vital organs like his heart and lungs were fine.

Human-Animal Rescue Bond

This is not the first time dolphins have been seen rescuing humans. Stories of dolphin rescues date back centuries. Today, the U.S. Navy has a marine mammal program. Just like police on land train dogs to find human bodies or drugs, Navy animal trainers teach dolphins to find items. At times, the Navy's trainers have worked with California sea lions, as well. These marine mammals are tenacious swimmers that can navigate through the ocean's depths much better than humans. Sea lions are good at marking spots for sailors and divers.

Dolphins use "echolocation," which is a way of sensing the movement of sound, to locate objects. One of their most important duties for the U.S. Navy's Marine Mammal Program (NMMP) is to find sea mines, which are weapons set to explode as ships pass over them. Dolphins can be trained to do this and have been used for this purpose since the 1980s. However, today the United States Navy is using more robots to locate the mines to avoid putting both humans and dolphins at risk.

Safety in the Surf

Even though it's a fun activity, surfing has a serious side. Beaches have different zones for swimming, surfing, and boating. It is important surfers stay in their zone. This protects everybody on the beach. Surfers should always wear a "leash" to keep the surfboard close and away from other people. Beginners should avoid crowded beaches when they are learning to surf. All surfers should listen to the lifeguard.

It is always important for surfers to check the weather and tide charts. Also, surfers should be on the lookout for sea creatures, such as sharks. Not only are some animals dangerous, but all surfers know they are sharing the ocean with sea animals.

When paddling out, a surfer should watch for people surfing atop incoming waves. The person riding the wave has the right of way. It is not safe to "snake." This is when one surfer "cuts" in front of another surfer on a wave. In a crowded area, a surfer should call out "right" or "left" to let others know which way he or she will be turning when dropping into a wave. Finally, surfers should take Basic First Aid classes so they can help others in an emergency. Each year, about three hundred of the 2 million Americans who surf are admitted to hospitals with injuries.

Helicopter Rodeo

Coast Guard helicopter pilots have a special way of practicing their flying skills. Each year, pilots at Air Station Astoria in Oregon stage a "helicopter rodeo." They form teams that compete with each other to do the best rescue stunts.

One event tests the team's ability to move an eight-hundred-pound steel ball from the end of an airstrip to a barrier on the other side. Another tests a pilot's ability to move a trail line into a barrel, and then drop six eggs into this same barrel from one hundred feet in the air.

"We got the steel ball from point 'A' to point 'B' but it hit the ground a few times, and every time it hits the ground you get time added to your score," said Petty Officer Third Class Adam Anderson. He is an electrician who spoke with U.S. Coast Guard reporters after the rodeo. "Of all the teams that went up, nobody got an egg in the barrel," said Anderson.

Even though the rodeo is fun for the pilots, it also helps them build skills important in carrying out rescue operations. Training Officer Lieutenant Mike Groncki said it increases the quality of teamwork among the crew members.

Operations Officer Lieutenant David Bartram was a member of the winning team in 2009. He said the rodeo helps pilots practice the kind of hovering that is often needed near cliffs. "We do a lot of that whether we're over the water or along a cliff face," Bartram said. He agreed the exercises build teamwork. Bartram and his teammates won twenty-four hours of "off duty" time and what are known as "bragging rights" among the other pilots as their prizes.

Words to Survive By

bow—The front part of a ship.

breaker—A wave that breaks into foam as it hits land on the shore.

cape—A strip of land that extends out into the water.

capsize—The overturning and head-first sinking of a ship.

cargo—Load of goods or people.

chamber—Room.

channel—A body of water joining two larger bodies of water.

chaplain—Pastor, minister, or clergy.

current—Water flowing in one direction.

domestic—Relating to the home or within one's home country.

emblem—A symbol of something or some group of people.

evacuation—Act of leaving or escaping.

executioner—A person who carries out a death sentence.

fanfare—A grand display of excitement, or a loud blowing of trumpets.

fleet—The number of warships under one person's or a country's command.

hostage—Person taken prisoner by an enemy.

hull—The frame, or main body of a ship.

intensive care—More than usual amount of attention, given to seriously ill patients.

mast—A vertical pole on a ship's top deck.

officer—The captain or authority aboard a ship or those with leadership training.

perish—To die.

port—A harbor where ships are launched or received.

quarters—Lodging, or room in which to stay.

ransom—Money traded for the release a prisoner.

reception—Party to greet guests.

salvage—Rescue of a ship and cargo.

skipper—The captain of a small ship.

sniper—A highly skilled shooter who can hit distant targets from a hidden place.

squall—A sudden storm that often brings strong wind and rain.

stern—The rear part of a ship.

submerge—To go underwater.

thermal—Clothing designed to keep heat from escaping.

vessel—Large ship.

Find Out More

Books

Gleason, Carrie. *Ocean Storm Alert*. New York: Crabtree Publishing Company, 2005.

Kuhne, Cecil, ed. *Near Death on the High Seas: True Stories of Disaster and Survival*. New York: Vintage Books, 2008.

Oliver, Clare. *Rescue At Sea*. London: Franklin Watts, 2002.

O'Shei, Tim. *How to Survive Being Lost at Sea*. Mankato, Minn.: Capstone Press, 2009.

Riley, Peter D. *Survivor's Science in the Ocean*. Chicago: Raintree, 2005.

Websites

Explore the *Mary Rose*

<http://www.maryrose.org/explore/index.htm>

United States Coast Guard

<http://www.uscg.mil/>

Ocean Rescue TV

<http://www.oceanrescue.tv/>

Index

Read Each Title in True Rescue Stories

TRUE MOUNTAIN RESCUE STORIES

Shocking and triumphant true accounts of railroad wre
plane and helicopter crashes, and mountaineers who nee
met their maker are featured in this collection.

ISBN: 978-0-7660-3572-7

TRUE OCEAN RESCUE STORIES

A naval ship lost in battle, a vessel wrecked by an iceberg,
even a surfer rescued by a family of dolphins are some of
exciting tales of struggle and survival that will keep you on
edge of your seat.

ISBN: 978-0-7760-3665-9

TRUE UNDERGROUND RESCUE STORIES

The harrowing tales of a baby trapped in a well, a man look
for caves in Kentucky, coal miners and gold miners pu
deadly predicaments, and a man rescuing another from
oncoming subway train.

ISBN: 978-0-7660-3676-5

TRUE WILDERNESS RESCUE STORIES

Read about thrilling rescues that took place in the wild, suc
how a person was saved from a burning forest fire, and ho
group of friends was rescued by their dog.

ISBN: 978-0-7660-3666-6